# BRANCH LINE TO LYNTON

Vic Mitchell and Keith Smith

*Cover picture: Cover: No. 761 Taw approaches Lynton in August 1935 and is signalled to enter the short bay platform. This was to be the last summer that trains would rattle and echo through the steep-sided Devon valleys. (H.F.Wheeller)*

*First published July 1992*
*Reprinted April 1993*

*ISBN 1 873793 04 9*

*Typesetting   - Barbara Mitchell*
*Design        - Deborah Goodridge*

*Published by Middleton Press*
          *Easebourne Lane*
          *Midhurst*
          *West Sussex*
          *GU29 9AZ*
          *Tel: (0730) 813169*

*Printed & bound by Biddles Ltd,*
          *Guildford and Kings Lynn*

# CONTENTS

# ACKNOWLEDGEMENTS

We are very grateful for the assistance received from the photographic comtributors and also from Mrs J.E.Baker, G.A.Brown, P.Bennett, R.M.Casserley, G.Croughton, F.Hornby, Dr.S.Huber, D.Hudson, B.Jones, A.Ll.Lambert, N.Langridge, D.Salter, G.T.V.Stacey, N.Stanyon, Miss M.Wheeller and our ever helpful wives.

Railways of the Exmoor area in 1935.
(Railway Magazine)

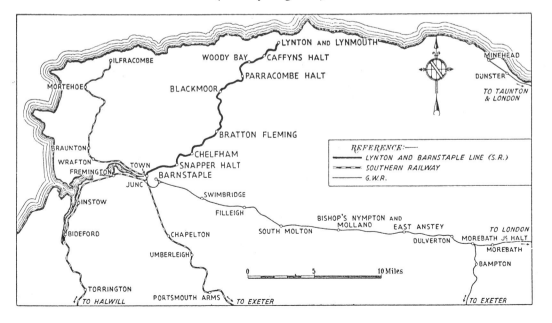

# GEOGRAPHICAL SETTING

The route followed the narrowing valley of the River Yeo from its mouth at Barnstaple to its source near Blackmoor Gate, traversing Pilton Shales before running onto a narrow exposure of Upcott Slates north of Chelfham. At Chelfham the line crossed a deep valley, incised by a small tributary of the Yeo, by means of an impressive curved viaduct.

In the vicinity of Bratton Fleming the railway was constructed on sandstone, while further north Grey Slates and Kentisbury Slates made the digging of cuttings difficult. Despite the optimism of the railway promoters, the slates of the district were of little economic importance.

Near Parracombe the line came onto an extensive area of Hangmans Grits on which it remained to within a mile of the terminus, this final section being downhill on Lynton Slates.

All the maps in this album are to the scale of 25" to 1 mile, unless otherwise indicated.

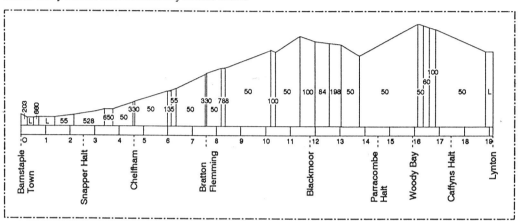

# HISTORICAL BACKGROUND

The London & South Western Railway train service from Exeter was extended north from Crediton to Barnstaple in 1854 and to Bideford in 1855. GWR trains reached Barnstaple (Victoria Road) from Taunton in 1873, the connecting spur to the LSWR opening in 1887. The Ilfracombe route came into use in 1874 and was operated by the LSWR. The first station on this branch was Barnstaple Quay, later renamed Barnstaple Town.

The upland mass of Exmoor was neglected by railway promoters, owing to its thinly scattered population, low agricultural productivity and difficult terrain. Eventually local entrepreneurs, led by Sir George Newnes, obtained an Act of Parliament on 27th June 1895, which authorised the construction of a narrow gauge (1ft 11½ins) line between Barnstaple and Lynton.

The optimistic prospectus resulted in the shares being oversubscribed but severe financial difficulties soon followed, due to extortionate prices demanded by landowners and lack of a geological survey. The latter resulted in the bankruptcy of the contractor, J. Nuttall.

The Lynton and Barnstaple Railway opened in its entirety for passengers and goods from a new station in Barnstaple on 16th May 1898. It struggled under financial difficulties, only paying a small dividend between 1913 and 1921. Negotiations for the sale of the railway to the LSWR took place in 1922. This was completed in March 1923, by which time the LSWR was part of the Southern Railway. (The line was not subject to the 1921 Railways Act, as narrow gauge or joint lines were not included in the "Grouping").

The SR carried out many improvements and promoted the line energetically but to no avail, as the effects of improved road transport were unbeatable. The last train ran on 29th September 1935 and the assets were auctioned on 13th November following.

Since the promoters declared that the line would resemble the Festiniog Railway, some similarities and differences will be mentioned in the captions.

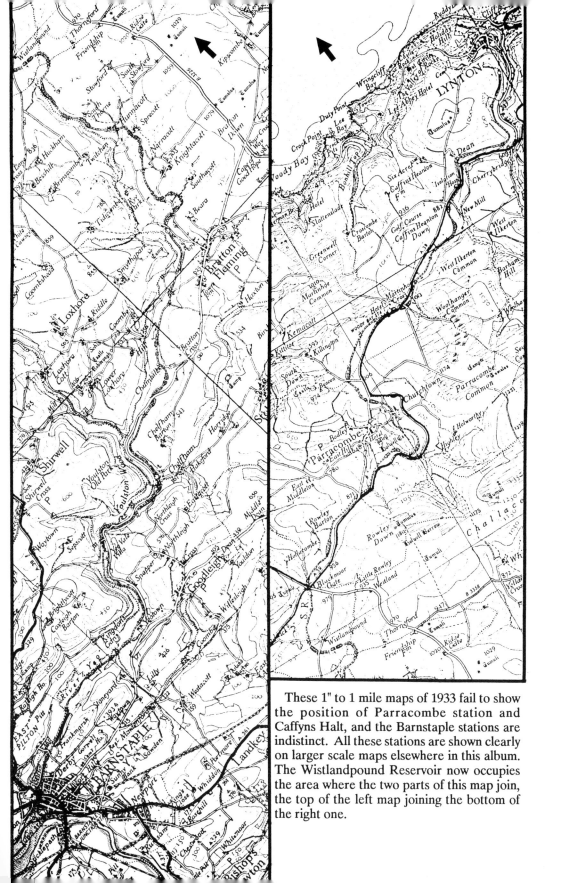

These 1" to 1 mile maps of 1933 fail to show the position of Parracombe station and Caffyns Halt, and the Barnstaple stations are indistinct. All these stations are shown clearly on larger scale maps elsewhere in this album. The Wistlandpound Reservoir now occupies the area where the two parts of this map join, the top of the left map joining the bottom of the right one.

1. The difficult terrain presented a challenge to the contractor, particularly as he naively believed that there was no rock below ground level. Over 80 bridges were required on the 19¼ mile route. (R.C.Riley coll.)

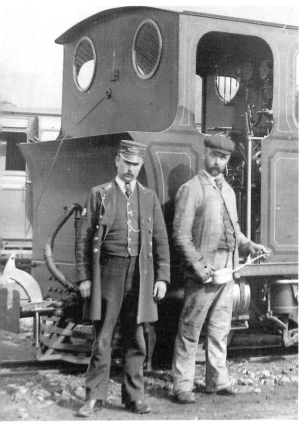

LYNTON & BARNSTAPLE RAILWAY,
SNAPPER PLATFORM
TO
BARNSTAPLE TOWN.
THIRD SINGLE – 3d.
This ticket must be given up when leaving
the Company's premises

2. In the early years there was a total staff of about 60 men, train operation being undertaken by three sets of crew. Note the coupling chain through the back plate of the cab of *Yeo*. (R.C.Riley coll.)

# ROLLING STOCK

The locomotives are described in the captions. the full technical specifications being listed in all other books on the line and therefore not repeated here.

Most of the seven different types of bogie coach are illustrated herein. The Bristol Wagon & Carriage Works supplied 16 vehicles to six designs, one more being constructed locally in 1903 and numbered 17.

Initially the freight fleet comprised 14 four-wheelers and 4 bogies, all painted light grey. By 1923 there were 13 open wagons, nine vans and two flat wagons. The SR provided four bogie vans, four bogie wagons, two cranes and a match truck. Built to the same high standard as the coaches, all these vehicles were fitted with vacuum brakes.

# PASSENGER SERVICES

Initially there were five weekday trains each way and one on Sundays. In the summer of 1898 only, there was a short working from Lynton at 10.30am to Blackmoor, returning from there at 11.15.

Until World War I, the winter weekday service comprised three trains and was increased to six in high summer, with transitional services in spring and autumn. On Sundays a single return trip was normally made. Additional trains were operated on Fridays in connection with Barnstaple Market, notably an early morning departure from Lynton. This necessitated an evening train from Barnstaple on Thursdays, the crew lodging out. An evening return trip was worked on Fridays and sometimes Saturdays in the summer.

During and after WWI, economies necessitated running a minimal basic service of three trains, with extras occasionally.

The takeover by the SR resulted in improvements of up to seven journeys in the summer and higher speeds following track improvements, although overall journey times were always poor, owing to the habit of shunting goods wagons at intermediate stations. From 1932, until closure, there were up to five trains in the winter timetable and six in the summer.

The appearance of bus times in the summer railway timetables from 1931 onwards was due to the fact that the SR had a large shareholding in Southern National, who later developed a transport monopoly in the area. Following closure of the railway, the bus frequency was increased to four journeys each weekday, the April 1992 timetable showing five, remarkable in view of the severe cuts elsewhere.

| ALL TRAINS PARLIAMENTARY | | | | | | | | | |
|---|---|---|---|---|---|---|---|---|---|
| **DOWN.—Week Days.** | a.m. | | a.m. | | a.m. | | p.m. | | p.m. | | | a.m. | |
| BARNSTAPLE (Town) ... ... .. dep. | 6 35 | ... | 8 46 | ... | 11 30 | ... | 3 45 | ... | 5 24 | ... | | 7 30 | ... |
| Chelfham .. .. .. ... ,, | 7 1 | ... | 9 9 | ... | 11 52 | ... | 4 8 | ... | 5 47 | ... | | 7 54 | ... |
| Bratton ... . .. ... ,, | 7 20 | ... | 9 25 | ... | 12 9 | ... | 4 27 | ... | 6 3 | ... | | 8 15 | ... |
| Blackmoor ... ... ,, | 7 45 | ... | 9 50 | ... | 12 31 | ... | 4 49 | ... | 6 28 | ... | | 8 40 | ... |
| Wooda Bay . ... .. ,, | 8 9 | ... | 10 11 | ... | 12 53 | ... | 5 10 | ... | 6 49 | ... | | 9 4 | ... |
| LYNTON .. ... .. .. arr. | 8 25 | ... | 10 28 | ... | 1 9 | ... | 5 26 | ... | 7 5 | ... | | 9 20 | ... |
| **UP.—Week Days.** | a.m. | | a.m. | | p.m. | | p.m. | | p.m. | | | p.m. | |
| LYNTON ... .. ... . dep. | 6 14 | ... | 9 10 | ... | 1 50 | ... | 3 25 | ... | 5 45 | .. | | 5 38 | ... |
| Wooda Bay ... ... ... ,, | 6 33 | ... | 9 28 | ... | 2 8 | ... | 3 43 | ... | 6 3 | ... | | 5 57 | ... |
| Blackmoor ... ... ... ,, | 6 58 | ... | 9 53 | ... | 2 31 | ... | 4 6 | ... | 6 28 | ... | | 6 22 | ... |
| Bratton .. ... ... ... ,, | 7 23 | ... | 10 15 | ... | 2 53 | ... | 4 31 | ... | 6 50 | ... | | 6 47 | ... |
| Chelfham ... ... ... ,, | 7 40 | ... | 10 29 | ... | 3 8 | ... | 4 46 | ... | 7 5 | ... | | 7 4 | ... |
| BARNSTAPLE (Town) ... ... . arr. | 8 2 | ... | 10 50 | ... | 3 30 | ... | 5 7 | ... | 7 26 | ... | | 7 26 | ... |

# BARNSTAPLE TOWN

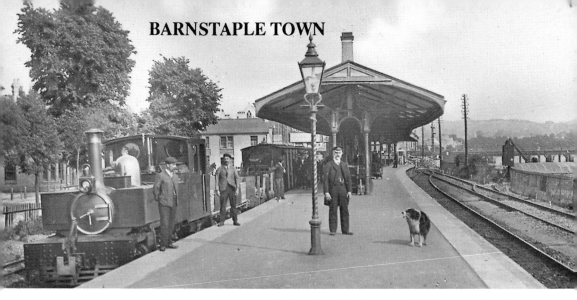

⟵

The 1932 edition at 6" to 1 mile has the 1873 GWR route lower right, with the 1887 connection across the bottom of the map. The 1854 line from Crediton is lower left. Diverging left at Barnstaple Junction is the Bideford line, the Ilfracombe route curving across the River Taw and passing through the Town station. The L&BR commences here and curves east, to run across the top of the map. Barnstaple Junction is now the terminus of the single line from Exeter and is known simply as "Barnstaple", all other tracks having been lifted.

3. On the right the curved bridge carrying the LSWR line from Barnstaple Junction is superimposed against Long Bridge, which carries the main road from the south. The level crossing at the far end of the platform was used by road traffic to the quay, the first station having been situated between it and the bridge. (D.Cullum coll.)

4. 2-6-2T *Exe* reverses into the station which opened with the L&BR on 11th May 1898. Its predecessor was 250 yds nearer to Long Bridge and was named "Barnstaple Quay" until becoming "Barnstaple Town" in July 1886. (R.C.Riley coll.)

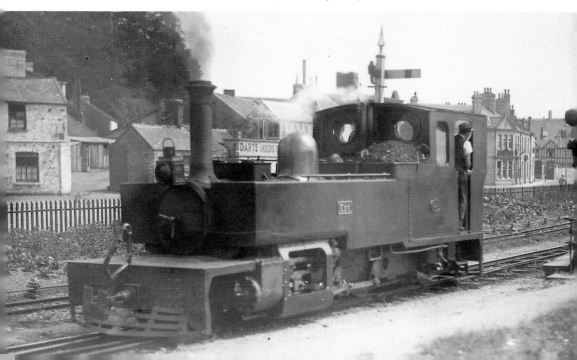

5. *Lew* and *Exe* wait to leave with a mixed train on 21st July 1925, the leading vehicle carrying hay. Sheeting of this commodity was necessary at all times to reduce the risk of conflagration from engine sparks. (H.C.Casserley)

6. The short siding at the end of the run-round loop was used for the short term storage of stock, most of it being kept at Pilton Depot. *Lyn* is seen prior to repainting in SR livery at Eastleigh in 1928. The ugly chimney replaced the original copper capped design prior to 1923. (Lens of Sutton)

The diamond hatching at the bottom of this 1906 map represents the glass canopy of Barnstaple Town station. The exchange sidings are lower left, while Pilton Yard and Depot of the L&BR is shown top right. Above Braunton Bridge is a narrow gauge siding, while downstream on the opposite bank is a much longer standard gauge line, both being for the transfer of sea-borne freight. The dots are along the centre of the meandering River Yeo. The narrow gauge siding is shown branching in the opposite direction on the previous map.

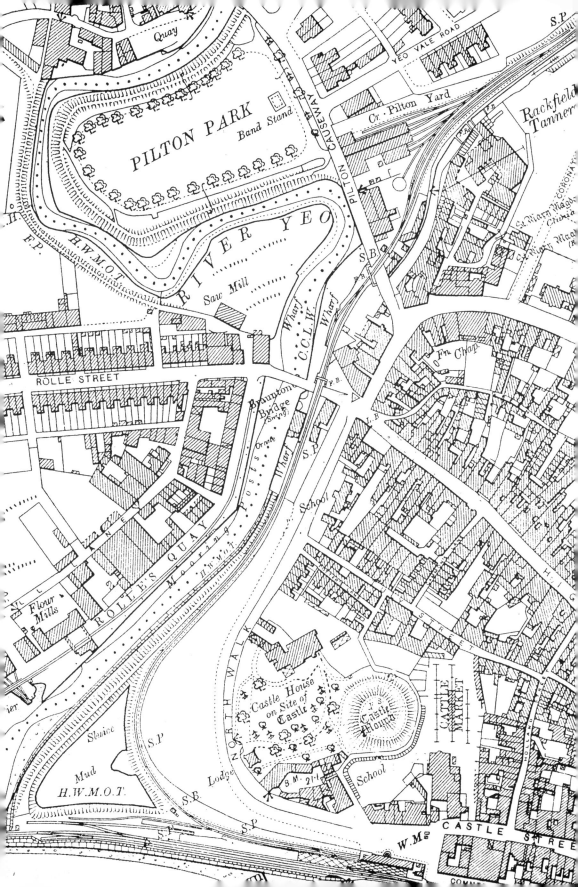

7. Not only did the SR repaint all the rolling stock but it provided steam heating in six of the carriages in 1933. The steam connection is to the left of *Taw's* coupling and vacuum brake pipe. (Lens of Sutton)

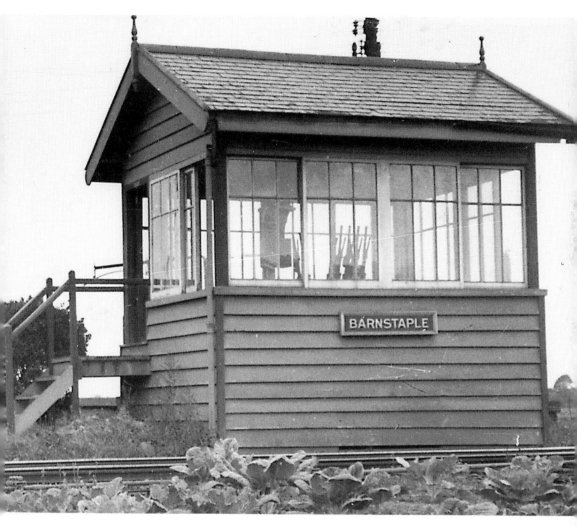

SOUTHERN RAILWAY.
This Ticket is issued subject to the Company's Bye-laws, Regulations & Conditions in their Time Tables, Notices and Book of Regulations.

EXCESS TICKET
Barnstaple Town to
**LYNTON**
CHANGE of CLASS THIRD to FIRST
Fare 1/7

NUMBER OF
ORIGINAL TICKET H 311

1767   1767

LYNTON & BARNSTAPLE Ry.
Lynton To
**BARNSTAPLE TOWN**
Lynton   Lynton
Barnstaple Tn   Barnstaple Tn
First   First
Class   Class
Fare 3/4   See Over   Fare 3/4

18 SP 18   7390

9. In contrast to the partly brick LSWR box at the east end of the station, the L&BR provided an all-timber structure. The LSWR signalman enjoyed a view of the estuary, while here the staff gazed at their own cabbages. This 1935 view shows most of the levers. (H.F.Wheeller)

8. Despite falling traffic, the SR supplied four new bogie vans to the line. They were built by J & F Howard of Bedford in 1927 on heavy frames with generous bracing and were of pleasing proportions when seen in a passenger train. The body bracing had originally been timber. (H.F.Wheeller)

10. Originally oil lit, the coaches had acetylene lighting for most of their lives. Clamped onto a small shelf is the generator which contained calcium carbide. A needle valve controlled a slow flow of water onto the compound, the resulting gas being piped up the end of the coach and to the adjacent coach via a flexible pipe, here obscured in the shadow. (R.Shepherd)

11. The crew of *Taw* pose oblivious to the "right-away", no doubt also posed. Chains retained the lids to the oil lamp housings, which remained in place for the gas lighting. There appears to be only three coaches in the formation. Four was the maximum for one locomotive. (Lens of Sutton)

12. This and the next three photographs were taken on the final day of operation, Sunday 29th September 1935. Still displaying its enormous headlamp, *Yeo* is not as clean as she appears in other views of happier days. (R.C.Riley coll.)

13. The shadow reminds us that the station was also gas lit, but this was coal gas piped from the gasworks near the GWR station in Victoria Road. Spray from the wheels has caused the rusty patch on coach no.2465, formerly no. 7. Seldom are stationmasters seen with a white hat cover. (R.C.Riley coll.)

14. *Lew* and *Yeo* wait to depart at 11.50 on the last morning of operation. There were reports of mourning all day. The exchange siding and its catch point are evident, as is the stump of the water column, by then only carrying a tap. (R.C.Riley coll.)

July 1906

### LYNTON and BARNSTAPLE.
Sec. and Man., Charles E. Drewett, Pilton Bridge, Barnstaple.

| Miles | | Week Days. | Sn | | Week Days. | Sn |
|---|---|---|---|---|---|---|
| | | mrn mrn mrn aft aft aft aft mrn | mrn | | mrn mrn mrn aft aft aft aft | aft |
| | Barnstaple Town...dep. | 6 20 9 5 1036 2 25 2 30 4 20 5 30 6 55 | 7 30 | Lynton..........dep. | 8 20 8 50 1045 1225 5 14 6 25 7 10 | 5 38 |
| 5 | Chelfham............. | 6 41 9 27 1050 2 46 3 50 4 40 5 50 7 15 | 7 52 | Woody Bay.......... | 8 36 9 6 11 1 1241 5 30 6 41 7 26 | 5 55 |
| 8 | Bratton Fleming...... | 6 57 9 44 11 5 3 4 2 4 4 56 4 7 29 8 7 | | Blackmoor........... | 8 55 9 25 1122 1259 5 48 7 1 7 46 | 6 14 |
| 12 | Blackmoor........... | 7 18 10 2 1123 3 21 4 24 5 12 6 22 7 47 8 26 | | Bratton Fleming..... | 9 12 9 43 1139 1 17 6 5 7 20 8 4 | 6 33 |
| 16 | Woody Bay........... | 7 38 1021 1142 3 40 4 43 5 32 6 42 8 7 6 8 46 | | Chelfham .......... | 9 26 9 58 1153 1 32 6 19 7 35 8 19 | 6 49 |
| 19½ | Lynton **..........arr. | 7 53 1036 1157 3 55 4 58 5 47 6 56 8 22 9 2 | | Barnstaple Tn. 43 ar | 9 45 1017 1211 1 52 6 37 7 54 8 38 | 7 9 |

All Trains stop at Snapper (for Goodleigh) Platform, also at Parracombe Platform to take up or set down on informing the Guard. **d** Wednesdays only. **g** Except Wednesdays. **h** Runs on 12th, 19th, and 26th instant. **i** Runs on 13th, 20th, and 27th instant. **\*\*** Station for Lynmouth.

15. No doubt the photographer forced a few smiles on the sad occasion. In the background is the largest radius point on the line, reputedly having been designed to permit passenger trains to start from the loop, had a second platform been necessary. (R.C.Riley coll.)

16. All the equipment, except some machine tools, was sold by auction on 13th November 1935. The track to milepost 15½ was acquired by S.Castle of Plymouth who used *Lew* and three wagons to bring the materials to the exchange siding, visible in the background. The remaining track was lifted quickly by the SR prior to the sale, presumably to forestall any attempts to reopen the line. (R.C.Riley coll.)

### BARNSTAPLE TOWN and LYNTON.—Lynton and Barnstaple.
Sec. and Man., Charles E. Drewett, Pilton Bridge, Barnstaple.

| | Down. | Week Days. | | | | Suns. | | | Up. | Week Days. | | | | Suns. |
|---|---|---|---|---|---|---|---|---|---|---|---|---|---|---|---|
| Miles | | mrn mrn | mrn aft | aft aft | | mrn | | Miles | | mrn mrn | aft aft | aft aft | | aft |
| | Barnstaple Town dep. | 6 20 8 55 | 1028 1 55 | 4 46 7 15 | | 7 30 | | | Lynton dep. | 8 10 10 43 | 1217 4 26 | 6 30 8 50 | | 5 38 |
| 5 | Chelfham | 6 39 9 15 | 1047 2 15 | 5 07 7 35 | | 7 50 | | 3¼ | Woody Bay | 8 25 10 59 | 1233 4 42 | 6 46 9 6 | | 5 54 |
| 8 | Bratton Fleming | 6 55 9 31 | 11 2 2 30 | 5 36 7 50 | | 8 5 | | 7¾ | Blackmoor | 8 43 11 19 | 1251 5 0 | 7 4 9 24 | | 6 12 |
| 12 | Blackmoor | 7 15 9 49 | 1120 2 49 | 5 34 8 7 | | 8 23 | | 11½ | Bratton Fleming | 9 6 11 36 | 1 8 5 17 | 7 21 9 41 | | 6 29 |
| 16 | Woody Bay | 7 34 10 8 | 1139 3 8 | 5 53 8 26 | | 8 42 | | 14½ | Chelfham | 1559 1411 51 | 1 23 5 32 | 7 36 9 55 | | 6 44 |
| 19¼ | Lynton arr. | 7 48 10 21 | 1153 3 22 | 6 7 8 40 | | 8 56 | | 19¼ | Barnstaple Town arr. | 9 32 12 9 | 1 41 5 50 | 7 54 1013 | | 7 2 |

†† Over ¼ mile to Barnstaple (G. W.).  ‡‡ Station for Lynmouth.
¶ "Halts" at Snapper (for Goodleigh), between Barnstaple Town and Chelfham, but during daylight only; and at Parracombe, between Blackmoor and Woody Bay.

**October 1914**

**August 1934**

### BARNSTAPLE TOWN and LYNTON AND LYNMOUTH.

| | Down. | Week Days | | | | | | Sn | aft | Up. | Week Days | | | | | | | Suns. | |
|---|---|---|---|---|---|---|---|---|---|---|---|---|---|---|---|---|---|---|---|
| Miles | | mrn mrn | mrn aft | aft aft | | S | aft | aft | | | mrn mrn | aft aft | aft aft | aft aft | | mrn aft | |
| | | | | | | J | F | J | | | | J | | | | J | J |
| | Barnstaple Town lp. | 533 7 0 | 1015 133 | 315 425 | 4 | 4 55 7 50 | 3 40 | | Lynton & Lynmth dep. | 7 13 9 25 | 1242 2 0 | 330 6 7 | 8 5 9 30 | | 9 30 1 25 | |
| 2½ | Snapper Halt | 544 | 1026 144 | 326 436 | | 8 1 | | | Caffyns Halt | 9 33 1250 | 338 615 | 8 13 9 38 | | | | |
| 5 | Chelfham | 1035 153 | 335 445 | 5 | 5 8 9 | 4 8 0 | | Woody Bay | 7 27 9 40 | 1257 2 17 | 345 622 | 8 20 9 45 | | 9 47 1 32 | |
| 8 | Bratton Fleming | 6 5 7 31 | 1050 2 8 | 349 459 | 5 35 8 23 | 4 25 | | Parracombe Halt | 7 34 9 48 | 1 5 2 22 | 353 630 | 8 28 9 54 | | 9 52 1 37 | |
| 12 | Blackmoor | 6 22 7 49 | 11 8 2 26 | 4 8 517 | 5 55 8 44 | 4 45 | | Blackmoor | 7 48 10 2 | 1 19 2 36 | 4 7 645 | 8 41 10 7 | | 10 0 2 0 | |
| 14½ | Parracombe Halt | 6 35 8 1 | 1121 2 40 | 421 531 | 6 3 8 55 | 4 53 | | Bratton Fleming | 8 7 10 20 | 1 37 2 56 | 425 7 2 | 8 58 1025 | | 10 20 2 25 | |
| 16 | Woody Bay | 6 43 8 9 | 1130 2 50 | 432 540 | 6 8 9 3 | 4 58 | | Chelfham | 8 20 1031 | 1 51 3 10 | 443 715 | 9 12 1038 | | 1040 2 45 | |
| 17½ | Caffyns Halt lmouth | 651 815 | 1139 259 | 441 548 | 9 11 | | | Snapper Halt 176,177 | 8 29 1044 | 2 2 | 455 728 | 9 20 1047 | | | |
| 19¼ | Lynton & Lyn arr. | 7 0 824 | 1148 3 8 | 450 557 | 6 25 920 | 5 15 | | Barnstaple Tn. G arr. | 8 41 1056 | 2 16 340 | 5 7 735 | 9 32 1059 | | 11 A 0 3 A 5 | |

A J a nstaple Junc. Sta.  B Chelfham Cross.  C Blackmoor Gate.
F Fris. and sats.  F Southern National Omnibus Office.  G Over ¼ mile to Barnstaple Sta.
J or J Southern National Motor Omnibus.  Times subject to alteration.
K Commences 22nd July.  L On 8th and 15th July only.  S Saturdays only.

17. Wagon no.28309 was photographed on 24th August 1936, by which time only the track to Pilton depot remained. This and four wagons remained until the summer of 1937. This view includes most of the run-round loop and an example of the road transport that helped to kill the line. (R.K.Cope/R.S.Carpenter)

18. By September 1937, no track remained. On the right is the buffer stop and the platform of the goods exchange siding and in the background is the chimney of the Corporation's electricity works which generated DC current. The platform canopy was reduced in length later. (R.C.Riley)

19. Passenger services to Ilfracombe ceased on 5th October 1970, following which the station remained derelict for many years. This 1992 view shows the building in use as an Indian restaurant, with a museum sign on the left. (V.Mitchell)

SOUTHERN RAILWAY.
This Ticket is issued subject to the Bye-laws
Regulations & Conditions stated in the
Company's Time Tables Bills & Notices
Available on day of issue only

LYNTON to
**BARNSTAPLE TOWN**

| Lynton | Lynton |
| Barnstaple Town | Barnstaple Town |
| 3rd CLASS | 3rd CLASS |
| Fare 2/6 | Fare 2/6 |

20. A lease on the signal box was acquired by the L&BR Association in 1987 and it was renovated to serve as a museum and shop. The aim is to reopen two or three miles of the L&B from the outskirts of Barnstaple and to this end a number of items of rolling stock have been obtained. These include Kerr Stuart 0-6-0T *Axe* and a number of diesel locomotives. (M.Turvey)

21. The museum contains a remarkable range of relics of the line, these being on view to the public on weekdays from March to October. The association's rolling stock is stored at a depot at Landkey, the collection including parts of some of the original coaches which are being reassembled. (M.Turvey)

22. Although published before, this print of *Yeo* being unloaded from a standard gauge wagon shows clearly the detail of the traversing jacks. Also evident is a near horizontal double handled screw jack and a length of bridge rail of considerable antiquity. (R.C.Riley coll.)

24. Soon after the opening of the line, the directors considered that a fourth engine would be desirable but were unable to order from Manning Wardle owing to a long delivery schedule. Thus a USA manufacturer was chosen and Baldwins supplied 2-4-2T *Lyn* in July 1898. She is seen being returned from Eastleigh in January 1929, after overhaul and repainting. No other locomotive left the line; only the boilers were sent to the works. (R.C.Riley coll.)

### January 1934

| | BARNSTAPLE TOWN and LYNTON AND LYNMOUTH. | | | | | | | | | | | | |
|---|---|---|---|---|---|---|---|---|---|---|---|---|---|
| **Miles.** | **Down.** | | **Week Days only.** | | | | **Miles.** | **Up.** | | **Week Days only.** | | | |
| | | mn | mn | mrn | aft | aft | | | | mn | mrn | aft | aft |
| | | | | | **B** | | | | | | | **B** | |
| | Barnstaple Town dp. | 533 | 7 0 | 1015 | 133 | 425 | | Lynton & Lynmth dep. | 713 | 9 25 | 1242 | 336 | 6 7 |
| 2¼ | Snapper Halt | 544 | | 1026 | 144 | 436 | 1½ | Caffyns Halt | | 9 33 | 1250 | 343 | 615 |
| 5 | Chelfin | 552 | | 1035 | 153 | 445 | 3½ | Woody Bay | 727 | 9 40 | 1257 | 350 | 622 |
| 8 | Bratton Fleming | 6 6 | 721 | 1050 | 2 8 | 459 | 4½ | Parracombe Halt | 735 | 9 48 | 1 5 | 358 | 631 |
| 12 | Blackmoor | 623 | 749 | 11 8 | 226 | 517 | 7½ | Blackmoor | 749 | 10 2 | 1 19 | 412 | 645 |
| 14¼ | Parracombe Halt | 636 | 8 1 | 1121 | 240 | 531 | 11½ | Bratton Fleming | 8 7 | 1020 | 1 37 | 430 | 7 3 |
| 16 | Woody Bay | 644 | 8 9 | 1130 | 250 | 540 | 14½ | Chelfham | 829 | 1034 | 1 51 | 444 | 717 |
| 17½ | Caffyns Halt (mouth) | 652 | 815 | 1139 | 259 | 548 | 16½ | Snapper Halt 176,177 | 839 | 1044 | 2 2 | 455 | 725 |
| 19½ | Lynton & Lyn- arr. | 7 0 | 824 | 1148 | 3 8 | 557 | 19½ | Barnstaple Tn. G arr. | 841 | 1056 | 2 16 | 5 7 | 737 |

**B** Mons., Weds., and Sats.  **G** Over ¼ mile to Barnstaple Sta.

23. The SR decided that a fifth locomotive was required and ordered another 2-6-2T from Manning Wardle, who had built the first three. *Lew* had no rear coal bunker and was transferred by steam crane on 30th July 1925. (Lens of Sutton)

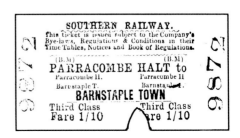

SOUTHERN RAILWAY.
This ticket is issued subject to the Company's Bye-laws, Regulations & Conditions in their Time Tables, Notices and Book of Regulations.
(B.M)  (B.M)
PARRACOMBE HALT to
Parracombe H.  Parracombe H
Barnstaple T.  Barnstaple T.
BARNSTAPLE TOWN
Third Class  Third Class
Fare 1/10  Fare 1/10

25. General goods received here from the main line was about eight times greater than that being transferred from the narrow gauge - hence the lower level of the latter. After closure, the L&B siding was raised to facilitate the off-loading of lifted track materials and a second siding was added. (D.Cullum coll.)

26. A complex telegraph pole stay system dominates this westward view, taken shortly before closure. The box in the centre distance is close to the swing bridge carrying the Ilfracombe line over the River Yeo. The standard gauge siding was lifted in April 1940. (R.Shepherd)

27. The last major transfer took place in 1936, when *Lew* was loaded for conveyance to Manning Wardles for overhaul prior to export to Brazil. Some redundant rails are stacked on the left. (E.Northcombe/R.C.Riley)

28. The crew seem reluctant to leave *Lew* as she is shunted into a local goods train. She bears metric weights for shipping and, despite intensive enquiries in recent years, has not been heard of since.
(E.Northcombe/R.C.Riley)

9952
SOUTHERN RAILWAY
CHEAP DAY
Available as advertised
Lynton to
BARNSTAPLE TOWN
Third Class    (S.6)
FOR CONDITIONS
SEE BACK.
SOUTHERN RAILWAY
CHEAP DAY
Available as advertised
B'staple To
Lynton
Barnstaple Town to
LYNTON
(S.6)   Third Class
9952

0260
SOUTHERN RAILWAY.
CHEAP DAY
Available as advertised
Lynton to
BARNSTAPLE
by Rail or Southern
National Omnibus.
Third Class
(Issued at Barnstaple Town).
FOR CONDITIONS
SEE BACK.
SOUTHERN RAILWAY.
CHEAP DAY
Available as advertised
Barnstaple T
by now
Barnstaple Town to
LYNTON
Third Class
4397

29. This and the following three pictures were taken in August 1936 to record the route of the line along the western edge of the town. Here is the down home signal and the coach seen in picture no.17. This area is now occupied by the Civic Centre and a police station. (R.K.Cope/R.S.Carpenter)

30. The hut seen in the previous picture also appears here to help link the two. Rolle's Quay is on the right, but its standard gauge siding is not evident. The concrete sleepers in this length were laid by the SR but their lack of resilience caused harsh and noisy riding. (R.K.Cope/R.S.Carpenter)

31. This northward view includes the concrete sleepers and tree seen in the previous picture but here the siding on Rolle's Quay is discernible. In the background is Braunton Bridge, which was rebuilt in 1978 with a fixed span. (R.K.Cope/R.S.Carpenter)

32. A closer view of the swing bridge includes the sand wharf, which was still in use in 1992. This is the end of the unpopular section of concrete sleepers. (R.K.Cope/R.S.Carpenter)

33. As on the Festiniog Railway, new management in the 1920s decided that cranes were required, in this case two. They were very little used, although one achieved fame after closure when it was used to demolish Braunton Road footbridge. The crossing gates (visible through the bridge) were the cause of a fatal accident in March 1910, when they were being opened by a platelayer. (R.C.Riley coll.)

34. Reference to the 25" map will confirm that the railway had a wharf north of Braunton Bridge. The contractor's locomotive *Excelsior* is near the site of the later siding. The leat to the mill on the right ran parallel to the railway in the vicinity of Pilton Depot, the outfall being through the arch on the right. A tidal defence wall, built in 1982-90, has transformed this scene and the mill has been replaced by a relief road. (R.C.Riley coll.)

35. After passing over the wharf siding points, trains ran under a footbridge (from which this photo was taken in 1936) and over Pilton Causeway level crossing, the gates of which are in the foreground. The points to the Pilton Depot loop are just beyond the signal box. (R.K.Cope/R.S.Carpenter)

36. An April 1992 view of the same location shows that the ornate gate post caps were retained when the posts were rebuilt with blocks and the gateway widened for lorry access. (V.Mitchell)

37. Initially the depot had a carriage shed (pitched roof) and a locomotive shed (curved roof). This is the scene on the opening day, with *Yeo* left (the first engine to be delivered) and *Exe* right. (Author's coll.)

BARNSTAPLE TOWN and LYNTON AND LYNMOUTH.—Southern (late Lynton and Barnstaple).

| Miles | Down. | Week Days only. | | | | | | | | Miles | Up. | Week Days only. | | | | | | |
|---|---|---|---|---|---|---|---|---|---|---|---|---|---|---|---|---|---|---|
| | | mrn | mrn | mrn | mrn | aft | aft | aft B | aft | | | mrn | mrn | mrn | aft | aft | aft | aft |
| | Barnstaple Town....dep | 6 20 | 7 5 | 8 45 | 1040 | 2 45 | 4 5 | 4 40 | 6 55 | | Lynton & Lynmouth dp | 8 5 | 9 10 | 1135 | 1240 | 4 25 | 6 15 | 8 35 |
| — | Snapper Halt............ | 6 30 | 7 15 | 8 55 | 1050 | 2 55 | 4 15 | 4 50 | 7 5 | — | Coffyus Halt............ | 8 11 | 9 18 | 1143 | 1248 | 4 33 | 6 23 | 8 43 |
| 5 | Chelfham ................. | 6 37 | 7 22 | 9 2 | 1059 | 3 2 | 4 22 | 4 57 | 7 12 | 3½ | Woody Bay ............ | 8 17 | 9 24 | 1150 | 1254 | 4 39 | 6 29 | 8 49 |
| 8 | Bratton Fleming......... | 6 52 | 7 37 | 9 19 | 1112 | 3 17 | 4 37 | 5 12 | 7 29 | — | Parracombe Halt....... | 8 24 | 9 31 | 1158 | 1 4 | 4 46 | 6 36 | 8 56 |
| 12 | Blackmoor.............. | 7 9 | 7 54 | 9 37 | 1129 | 3 34 | 4 54 | 5 31 | 7 46 | 7½ | Blackmoor.............. | 8 34 | 9 41 | 12 8 | 1 11 | 4 56 | 6 46 | 9 6 |
| — | Parracombe Halt......... | 7 24 | 8 9 | 9 54 | 1143 | 3 47 | 5 9 | 5 45 | 8 0 | 11½ | Bratton Fleming....... | 8 50 | 9 58 | 1234 | 1 27 | 5 13 | 7 2 | 9 23 |
| 16 | Woody Bay ............. | 7 30 | 8 15 | 10 0 | 1149 | 3 53 | 5 15 | 5 51 | 8 6 | 14½ | Chelfham ............... | 9 3 | 1011 | 1236 | 1 39 | 5 25 | 7 14 | 9 35 |
| — | Coffyus Halt............. | 7 38 | 8 24 | 10 7 | 1155 | 4 0 | 5 22 | 5 58 | 8 13 | — | Snapper Halt.....[above | 9 11 | 1019 | 1244 | 1 47 | 5 33 | 7 22 | 9 43 |
| 19½ | Lynton & Lynmouth arr. | 7 45 | 8 31 | 1014 | 12 5 | 4 7 | 5 29 | 6 5 | 8 20 | 19½ | Barnstaple Town ‖ arr | 9 20 | 1028 | 1253 | 1 56 | 5 42 | 7 31 | 9 52 |

B Fridays and Saturdays.      ‖ Over ¼ mile to Barnstaple (G.W.).

July 1924

38. The curved roof probably had rolled steel trusses which corroded quickly, as at Exmouth Junction. For much of its life the engine shed had a pitched tiled roof on timber frames. *Exe* is seen with the 12.31pm from Barnstaple on 28th August 1920, the engine shed being behind the leading coach. (K.Nunn/LCGB)

39. The sole 2-4-2T *Lyn* retained its American features to the end. Its square-windowed wooden cab was of no value to the scrap metal merchants and so it was acquired by an engineman for use as a garden shed. Seen in 1920, the livery was then holly green with black lining and the locomotive had not yet received the plain chimney seen in picture 24. (K.Nunn/LCGB)

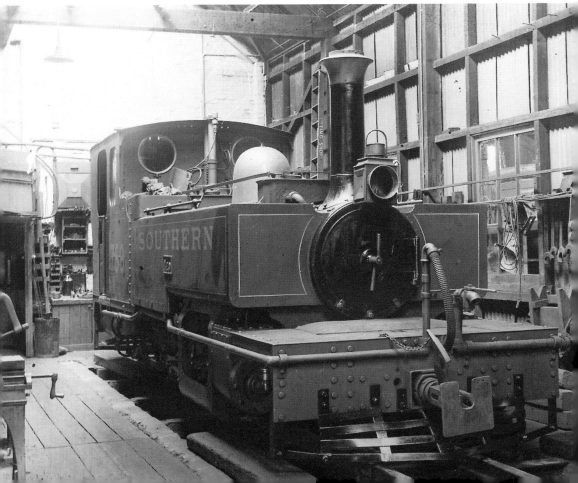

40. The L&B modified the cabs by moving the rear cab plate over the coal bunker. *Taw* is seen passing the water column with the 12.40 from Lynton in October 1926, before the locomotive was repainted by the SR.
(R.C.Riley coll.)

42. The northern part of the yard was devoted to goods traffic, one of the two goods sidings entering the shed on the right. Local traffic was handled here, in addittion to freight to and from the GWR, which was taken by road through the town. The crane (left) had a 16ft. jib and was rated at 10cwt. capacity.
(R.C.Riley coll.)

SOUTHERN RAILWAY.
This ticket is issued subject to the Company's Bye-laws, Regulations & Conditions in their Time Tables, Notices and Book of Regulations.
(No.2)                    (No.2)
BRATTON FLEMING  to
Bratton Fleming        Bratton Fleming
Barnstaple T.            Barnstaple T.
BARNSTAPLE TOWN
Third Class              Third Class
Fare 1/-                 Fare 1/-
The Passenger is requested to see this ticket punched at the time of issue

41. The more northerly of the two engine shed roads ran through into this well furnished workshop. *Yeo* stands over the pit and adjacent to the power hacksaw. Major boiler work was one task that could not be undertaken here. Beyond the window is the carriage repair shop. (Lens of Sutton)

LYNTON & BARNSTAPLE Ry.
Lynton  To      S.R
BARNSTAPLE TOWN
Lynton
Barnstaple T.
Third
Class
Fare 1/7½

43. The short wheelbase of *Lew* is evident in this 1935 view, which includes its maker's plate showing no.2042. Also clear in this picture are the vacuum brake reservoir and the oil drip tray under the slide bars. (S.W.Baker)

45. Disposal of locomotives took place on the south side of the shed where the coaling crane was located. In the early years 200-300 tons of coal would arrive at the nearby wharf but this was mainly for a coal merchant at Lynton. Locomotive coal was normally received in 10-ton batches via the LSWR. (Lens of Sutton)

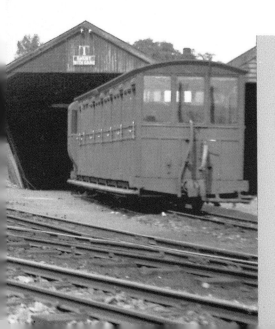

44. Within 12 months of the opening, the space between the two sheds was roofed over to create a carriage repair shop, its gable bearing a notice "*I SHUNT WITH CARE*". *Taw* takes the down loop with the 10.15am on 15th June 1935, passing one of the saloon observation coaches. (S.W.Baker)

*Postscript.* After this volume was completed, this splendid aerial view from about 1923 was discovered. It is therefore included here as a reminder that Pilton Depot was the nerve centre of the L&B and that the efficiency and competence of its staff made every journey a safe and pleasurable experience.
(R.L.Knight/K.Skinley)

46. An historic day in the life of the line was 13th November 1935, when the assets were auctioned. *Lew* fetched £52, *Yeo* and *Taw* £50 each and Exe only £34, as she had a steel firebox. Seen here is *Lyn* which raised £50, but numerous spares were included in the lot. (R.C.Riley coll.)

⟶

48. Lot 16 was coach no.6992 (originally no.2) which contained 1st and 3rd class compartments, 1st class observation saloon, luggage and guard's sections. It was photographed prior to transport to Clannaborough Rectory at Challacombe, three miles east of Blackmoor. (R.C.Riley coll.)

47. Many of the wagons had their bodies removed and the frames were shipped to Brazil with *Lew*. The turntable (marked on the map) was used mainly for turning vehicles to ensure even wheel and bearing wear. It was bought at the sale by the Romney, Hythe and Dymchurch Railway. (Lens of Sutton)

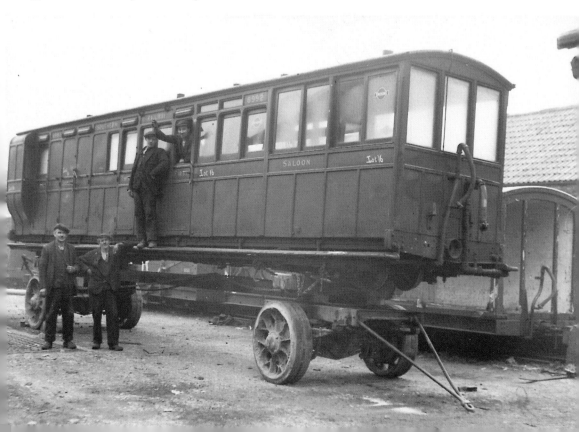

49. No.6992 gave pleasure to visiting clergy and others for many years. The interior was retained intact and in 1982 the body was conveyed to the National Railway Museum, where it was still awaiting restoration funds ten years later. This is the view of the first class compartment from the observation saloon. (R.C.Riley coll.)

51. The west elevation of the depot buildings are seen from Pilton Causeway in April 1992. From left to right their uses then and their former uses were road parcels service (goods shed), furniture store (carriage shed), timber merchant (carriage repair shop) and motor vehicle repairs (engine shed - east end). All later uses had some association with their original function. (V.Mitchell)

50. A number of locomotive relics were taken to Eastleigh and are seen on display in the paint shop in August 1938. Some nameplates went to York Railway Museum and others were acquired privately but are now secure public property. (S.W.Baker)

52. Opened in 1903, the halt was close to Yeotown, Snapper being the name of a former inn further north. Nearly a mile east was the village of Goodleigh, this being the main source of passenger traffic here.
(Lens of Sutton)

SOUTHERN RAILWAY.
This ticket is issued subject to the Company's Bye-laws, Regulations & Conditions in their Time Tables, Notices and Book of Regulations.
(No.4) Caffyns Halt to (No.4)
Caffyns Halt
Lynton
**LYNTON**
Third Class        Third Class
Fare 3d             Fare 3d
The Passenger is requested to see this ticket punched at the time of issue

53. The line ran east through the halt and then turned north past the houses of the Snapper district, visible in the distance. The route was climbing at 1 in 528 in this area.
(Lens of Sutton)

54.  Coach no.6991 (originally no.1) was sold with running gear and left on a short length of track in the platform. Seen in May 1937, the vehicle served agricultural purposes until being burnt in the 1960s. (S.W.Baker)

55.  No.6993 (no.15 initially) was left on rails north of the halt and was usually occupied by hens until removed to the Festiniog Railway in 1959. The bogies were repaired, the body reprofiled and it was fitted out as a buffet car. The Yeo valley narrows at Snapper and the scenery becomes progressively more impressive. (S.W.Baker)

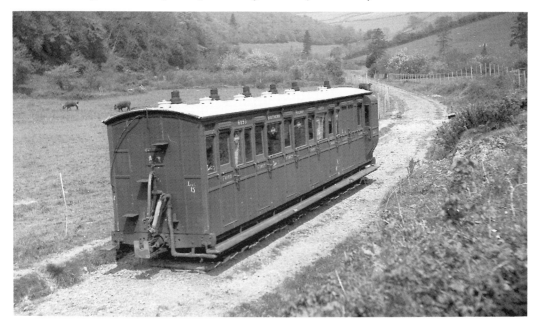

# CHELFHAM VIADUCT

56. Owing to the presence of a deep valley formed by a tributary of the Yeo, a 70ft. high viaduct was necessary. A steam crane on trestles was in use whereas within a few years aerial ropeways were in use - see our *Branch Line to Lyme Regis* picture 61. (R.C.Riley coll.)

57. *Slave* and *Kilmarnock* were two of the contractor's locomotives in use and are seen with a test train in February 1897. A deflection test was made later with 110 men and 28 wagons loaded with earth. (R.C.Riley coll.)

58. The eight spans gave a length of 112 yds and a good opportunity to view the scenery after the iron railings had been removed. Trains of up to nine coaches were permitted if double headed. (Lens of Sutton)

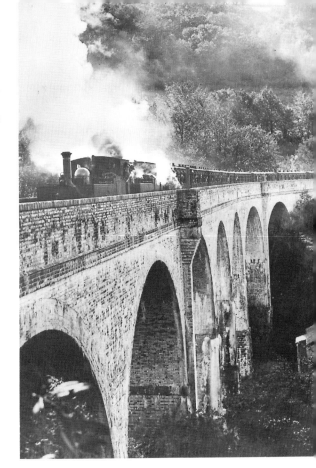

59. The east side is seen in 1964 from a point close to the station drive gates, the concrete posts of which were still in use in 1992. The parapet walls had been removed and the structure was still the responsibility of British Rail. The mill buildings have been incorporated into a school. (R.C.Riley)

# CHELFHAM

60. Both up signals are included in a postcard view of this delightful and peaceful location. The down starting signal is partially obscured by the water tank, when viewed from ground level. Note that the siding passes through the down platform edging. (R.C.Riley coll.)

61. The down home signal is beyond the viaduct and off, ready for the arrival of a train for Lynton. *Lew* will then pass over the unboarded crossing provided for access to the minute goods yard.
(A.B.MacLeod/D.Cullum coll.)

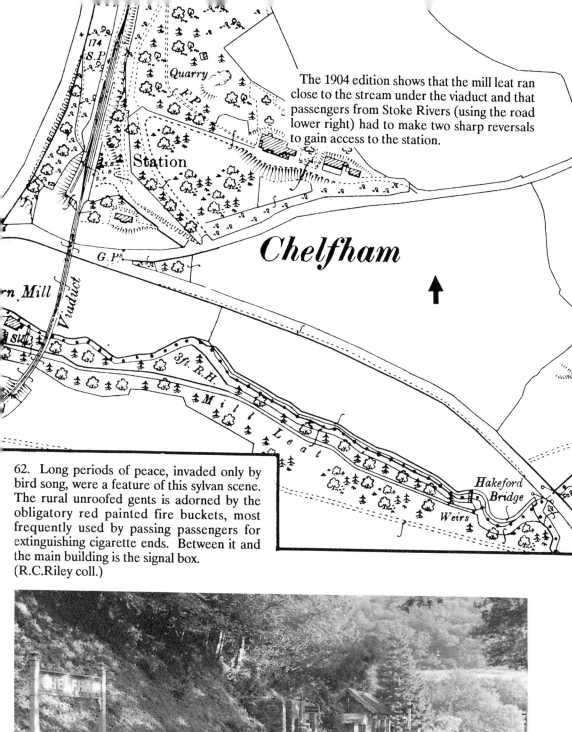

The 1904 edition shows that the mill leat ran close to the stream under the viaduct and that passengers from Stoke Rivers (using the road lower right) had to make two sharp reversals to gain access to the station.

62. Long periods of peace, invaded only by bird song, were a feature of this sylvan scene. The rural unroofed gents is adorned by the obligatory red painted fire buckets, most frequently used by passing passengers for extinguishing cigarette ends. Between it and the main building is the signal box. (R.C.Riley coll.)

63. *Taw* leaves the viaduct on 17th July 1935, only weeks before closure. The 1 in 50 gradient that she has just climbed is indicated by the fence posts in the background. Beyond the buffer stop on the right is a drop of over 50ft. to the valley floor. (S.W.Baker)

64. The box contained seven levers in a knee frame. In the final year trains crossed here at about 10.35am and 1.52pm. At the intermediate stations, the Tyer's single line tablet instrument was located in the booking office. (H.F.Wheeller)

65. The main building contained a waiting room and booking office and was built of stone by Nuttall, the contractor for the line. A handsome porch provided an entrance on the east elevation. Note the GPO letter box for the convenience of passengers. (H.F.Wheeller)

### BARNSTAPLE TOWN and LYNTON.—Lynton and Barnstaple.

Sec. and Man., Charles E. Drewett, Pilton Bridge, Barnstaple.

| Miles | Down. | Week Days. | | | Suns. | Miles | Up. | Week Days. | | | Suns. |
|---|---|---|---|---|---|---|---|---|---|---|---|
| | | mrn mrn | mrn aft aft | | mrn | | | mrn mrn | aft aft aft | | aft |
| | Barnstaple Town ¶ dep. | 6 20 8 35 | 10 38 4 40 6 45 | | 7 30 | | Lynton ........ dep. | 5 20 10 20 | 12 25 6 30 8 20 | | 5 38 |
| 5 | Chelfham ........... | 6 39 8 54 | 10 57 5 07 4 | | 7 50 | 3¼ | Woody Bay ¶ ....... | 8 35 10 36 | 12 41 6 46 8 36 | | 5 54 |
| 8 | Bratton Fleming .... | 6 55 9 9 | 11 15 5 16 7 20 | | 8 5 | 7¾ | Blackmoor ......... | 8 53 10 55 | 12 59 7 4 8 54 | | 6 12 |
| 12 | Blackmoor ¶ ........ | 7 15 9 27 | 11 30 5 34 7 37 | | 8 23 | 11¼ | Bratton Fleming ..... | 9 10 11 12 | 1 16 7 21 9 11 | | 6 29 |
| 16 | Woody Bay ......... | 7 34 9 46 | 11 49 5 53 7 56 | | 8 42 | 14 | Chelfham ¶ .....[1 49] | 9 24 11 27 | 1 31 7 36 9 25 | | 6 44 |
| 19¼ | Lynton ‡‡ ...... arr. | 7 43 10 0 | 12 36 7 8 10 | | 8 56 | 19¼ | Barnstaple Town ‡† arr. | 9 42 11 45 | 1 49 7 54 9 43 | | 7 2 |

†† Over ½ mile to Barnstaple (G. W.).  ‡‡ Station for Lynmouth.

¶ "Halts" at Snapper (for Goodleigh), between Barnstaple Town and Chelfham, but during daylight only: and at Parracombe, between Blackmoor and Woody Bay.

February 1917

66. A 1937 view includes the top of the viaduct, which is now a listed structure and cannot therefore be demolished. The station has been converted to a dwelling and the surrounding land is now private property. (S.W.Baker)

67. Four men were travelling under gravity on a wagon loaded with ballast on 26th March 1913 when it left the rails near Chumhill. Sadly two died. No passengers suffered death or injury during the life of the line, a fine record. (R.C.Riley coll.)

68. Approaching Bratton Fleming the line crossed Lancey Brook Viaduct, which was 28ft high, 140ft long and comprised eight steel spans on masonry piers. (S.W.Baker)

# BRATTON FLEMING

69. The stone building was similar to that at Chelfham but the entrance porch was on the end instead of the road side. A hipped roof was another difference. Access was by way of the steeply inclined drive on the right, behind the small signal box. After closure, the station with two acres of land was sold for £100. (Lens of Sutton)

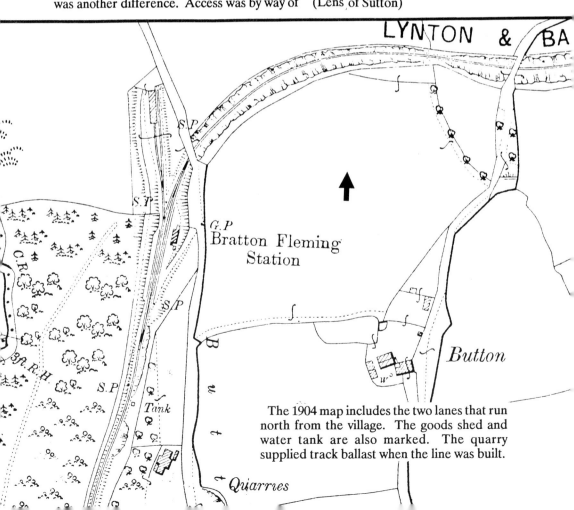

The 1904 map includes the two lanes that run north from the village. The goods shed and water tank are also marked. The quarry supplied track ballast when the line was built.

70. A view from the road bridge emphasises the steepness of the valley side. Weary shoppers returning from Barnstaple to the village had a vertical rise of 160ft to contend with. As at Chelfham, the siding passed through the down platform face. The population of the village dropped from 511 in 1901 to 442 in 1931. (Lens of Sutton)

71. In February 1932 the loop and one siding were removed and the remaining siding connected to the main line, as evident here. Also visible is the water tank which was little used as most down locomotives took water at Chelfham, moreover the train would have stood outside the station. (R.C.Riley coll.)

72. The steeply inclined road from the village passed over the bridge (which still exists in 1992) and reached rail level at the end of the sidings, where a gate to the yard was provided. To achieve this ideal, the sidings diverged sharply from the main line. This view of the goods shed was taken after the loop had been removed. (A.B.MacLeod/R.C.Riley)

73. A bay window and lean-to have been added, and the dwelling named *Long Acre*. The area is private but SR concrete fence posts can be seen from the road, these giving an indication of the former extent of railway property. (N.W.Hearn)

74. North of Bratton Fleming, a private 7¼" gauge railway has been laid on the old trackbed for about ½ mile. One mile east of the village a public 12¼" gauge railway has been built at Cape of Good Hope Farm, part of the one mile route being seen here with 2-8-0T *Yeo Valley*. The line opened in 1991 and in 1992 0-6-0T *Lorna Doone* was completed. (M.Turvey)

### October 1911

**BARNSTAPLE TOWN and LYNTON.—Lynton and Barnstaple.**
Sec. and Man., Charles E. Drewett, Pilton Bridge, Barnstaple.

| Miles | Down. | mrn | c | mrn | d | aft | aft | Fridays | Sundays mrn |
|---|---|---|---|---|---|---|---|---|---|
| | Barnstaple Town ¶ dep. | 6 20 | 9 5 | 10 30 | 12 38 | 4 40 | 6 53 | | 7 30 |
| 5 | Chelfham | 6 40 | 9 25 | 10 50 | 12 58 | 5 17 | 7 12 | | 7 50 |
| 8 | Bratton Fleming | 6 57 | 9 42 | 11 5 | 1 15 | 5 17 | 7 27 | | 8 5 |
| 12 | Blackmoor ¶ | 7 18 | 10 0 | 11 23 | 1 31 | 5 35 | 7 44 | | 8 23 |
| 16 | Woody Bay | 7 38 | 10 19 | 11 42 | 1 50 | 5 55 | 8 2 | | 8 42 |
| 19½ | Lynton ‡‡ arr. | 7 53 | 10 34 | 11 57 | 2 4 | 6 10 | 8 17 | | 8 57 |

| Miles | Up. | mrn | c | aft | d | aft | aft | Fridays | Suns. aft |
|---|---|---|---|---|---|---|---|---|---|
| | Lynton dep. | 8 20 | 10 45 | 12 20 | 3 50 | 6 30 | 8 25 | | 5 38 |
| 3½ | Woody Bay ¶ | 8 35 | 11 1 | 12 36 | 4 6 | 6 46 | 8 40 | | 5 54 |
| 7½ | Blackmoor | 8 53 | 11 22 | 12 54 | 4 25 | 7 6 | 8 58 | | 6 12 |
| 11½ | Bratton Fleming | 9 10 | 11 39 | 1 12 | 4 44 | 7 26 | 9 15 | | 6 29 |
| 14½ | Chelfham ¶ | 5 3 | 9 24 | 11 53 | 1 27 | 5 0 | 7 40 | 9 30 | 6 44 |
| 19½ | Barnstaple Town ‡† arr. | 9 42 | 12 11 | 1 46 | 5 19 | 7 58 | 9 49 | | 7 3 |

c Mondays, Wednesdays, and Fridays.   d Tuesdays, Thursdays, and Saturdays.
†† Over ¼ mile to Barnstaple (G.W.).   ‡‡ Station for Lynmouth.
¶ "Halts" at Snapper (for Goodleigh), between Barnstaple Town and Chelfham, but during daylight only; and at Parracombe, between Blackmoor and Woody Bay.

75. The station was situated at a cross roads on the moor, 900ft above sea level and remote from any villages. The roads, however, gave good communication with a considerable number of farms. This is the water column at the south end of the station, the tank being visible in the background. (Lens of Sutton)

76. *Lyn* has just taken water and is about to leave for Lynton. A hot air engine pumped water into the tank, its exhaust apparently projecting from the near window. More concrete sleepers are in evidence. Above the number is the letter E, indicating that maintenance was the responsibility of Eastleigh Works. (Lens of Sutton)

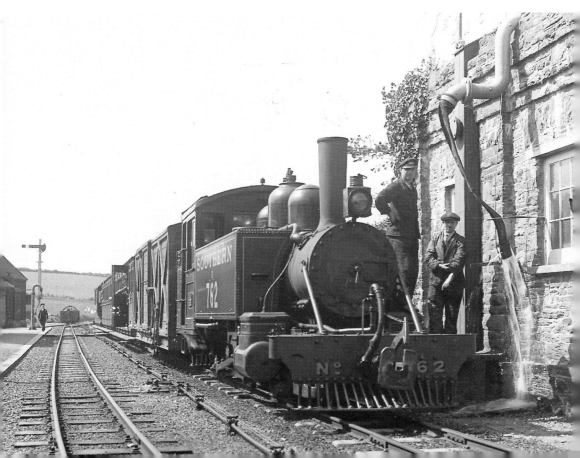

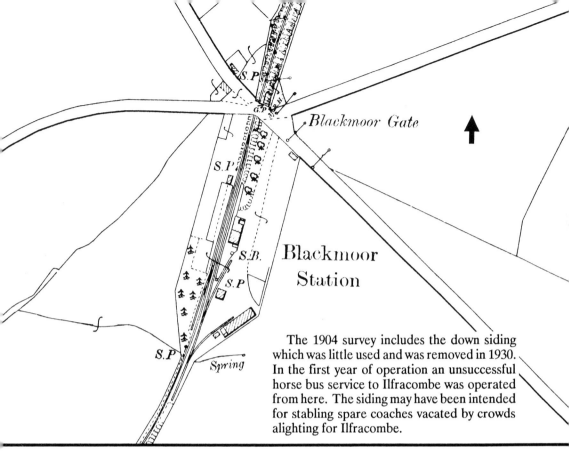

Blackmoor Gate

### Blackmoor Station

The 1904 survey includes the down siding which was little used and was removed in 1930. In the first year of operation an unsuccessful horse bus service to Ilfracombe was operated from here. The siding may have been intended for stabling spare coaches vacated by crowds alighting for Ilfracombe.

77. The cylinder drain cocks hiss as *Exe* departs for Lynton, the leading coach being one of four to have centre unglazed observation compartments for 3rd class tourists. The E above the engine numbers was not carried after 1931. (R.C.Riley coll.)

78. A 1931 view of passing trains includes the point rodding running between the foot crossing timbers. No facing point locks were provided but the signals were interlocked with the points at the lineside.
(P.J.Garland/R.S.Carpenter coll.)

79. *Yeo* obscures the small signal box but only part of the chalet type station. Lynton and Lynmouth were advertised as the Switzerland of England and so presumably the stations were of an appropriate style. This is July 1935. (S.W.Baker)

80. As at the previous two stations, a non-complementary hut was provided for the signal frame. An unusual and economical form of buffer stop is also shown. Unlike the FR, *down* trains climbed *up* for most of the journey. (H.F.Wheeller)

81. The buildings here, at Woody Bay and at Lynton, were built by Jones Bros of Lynton. A refreshment room was included, as was staff living accommodation. Beyond are the goods shed and the stables. A Milnes-Daimler motor bus was tried on the Ilfracombe service in 1903 but soon sold to the GWR owing to trouble with the police over speeding, in excess of 8mph. (S.W.Baker)

82. As on the Festiniog Railway, the route was severed after closure by the construction of a lake. Wistlandpound Reservoir has flooded the trackbed one mile south of the station. This 1992 view shows the "Old Station House Inn", the base of the water tower, a replica signal on the wrong side of the post and part of the water pipe. Behind the camera the bridge has gone, following road improvements. (V.Mitchell)

# SOUTH OF PARRACOMBE

**SOUTHERN RAILWAY.**
This ticket is issued subject to the Company's Bye-laws, Regulations & Conditions in their Time Tables, Notices and Book of Regulations.
**Blackmoor to**
Blackmoor Parracombe Halt — Blackmoor Parracombe Halt
**PARRACOMBE HALT**
Third Class Fare 4½d — Third Class Fare 4½d
2466    2466

**SOUTHERN RAILWAY.**
This Ticket is issued subject to the By-laws Regulations & Conditions stated in the Company's Time Tables Bills & Notices
Available on day of issue only
**BLACKMOOR to**
**PARRACOMBE HALT**
Blackmoor Parracombe Halt — Blackmoor Parracombe Halt
3rd CLASS — 3rd CLASS
Fare 4d — Fare 4d
846

83. A Lynton bound train in 1935 brakes hard as it descends the 1 in 50 to the bridge over the River Heddon. After crossing this it will rush to climb the 1 in 50 to Parracombe Halt. The nearby St. Petrock's Church is on the skyline. As on the Festiniog, one curve leads into another for most of the way. (S.W.Baker)

# PARRACOMBE

The 1903 revision at 6" to 1 mile has the main road (now A39) as a broad dark line with the railway roughly parallel and to the left of it. The halt is incorrectly marked "Parracombe Siding", the village being in a deep valley 120ft lower. Unusually, there are two substantial churches within a half mile.

84. The platform shelter is adjacent to the middle coach as a down train stops to take water from the unusual tank, the others seen so far being constructed of cast iron panels. The lane from this bridge to the A39 was still unsurfaced in 1992 and the shelter was still standing. (A.B.MacLeod/R.C.Riley)

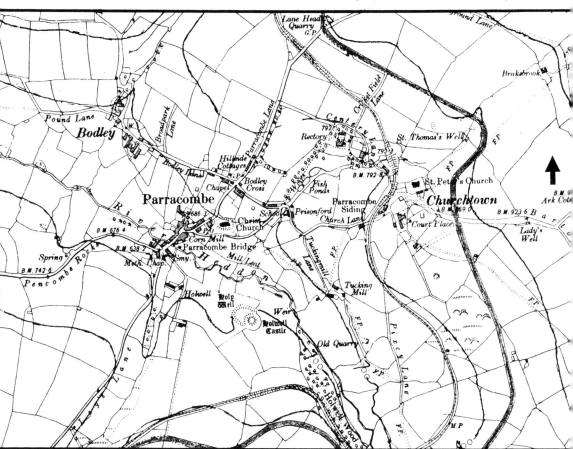

SOUTHERN RAILWAY.
Available on DAY of issue ONLY.
Lynton to
**PADDINGTON**
Via Barnstaple G.W.R. & Somerton or Bristol
THIRD CLASS
Issued in exchange for Return Half of Period Return ticket, issued by London Coastal Coaches Ltd. upon payment of the supplementary charge of 8/-
**FOR CONDITIONS SEE BACK.**

85. Initially trains were allowed to call here on Fridays only. The SR replaced the original wooden shelter with this concrete structure, probably large enough to serve a village of around 300 souls. For many years tickets were obtainable at the local post office. In 1992 a railway walk and an extensive 0 gauge garden railway were open to the public, north of the bridge. (Lens of Sutton)

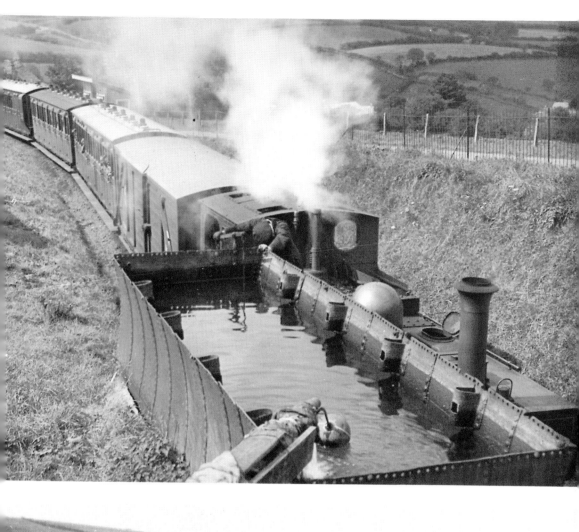

86. Until 1901 the station was listed as "Wooda Bay", its main purpose being to encourage residential and tourist developments around the bay, 1½ miles to the north. The contractor's locomotive *Slave* is hauling a mobile privy and timber bolsters coupled by ropes. (R.C.Riley coll.)

87. On 16th March 1898, *Yeo* waits with a press inspection party at this windswept location which is close to the summit of the line, 980ft above sea level. The anticipated building developments never took place and the station remained at an isolated cross roads known as Martinhoe Cross. The Festiniog Railway achieves an altitude of only 700ft. (R.C.Riley coll.)

88. A substantial hotel was built facing the station building but it remained in solitary isolation. Initially named the "Station Hotel", it eventually became the "Moorland Hotel", and more recently was converted to holiday flats. The station is now a private house. (Lens of Sutton)

The

# Moorland Hotel,

Woody Bay,

Parracombe, N. Devon.

'Phone: Parracombe 24.

## .. Tariff ..

| | |
|---|---|
| Breakfast – – | from 2/- |
| Cold Lunch – | ,, 2/- |
| Cold Lunch, with sweets | ,, 2/6 |
| Tea, plain – – | ,, 9d. |
| Tea, with cream | ,, 1/3 |
| Dinner – – – | 3/- |
| Bed and Breakfast each person | 5/6 |
| Early morning cup of Tea 3d. | |

From 9/- per day.

## .. Baths ..

| | |
|---|---|
| Hot – – – – | 1/- |
| Cold – – – – | 6d. |

Hot & Cold Water in all rooms.

Electric Light.

## .. Garage ..

| | |
|---|---|
| Cars – – per night | 1/- |
| Combinations & Motor Cycles | 6d. |

1938

89. Similar to Blackmoor in design, the building was much larger than traffic ever required. Through the cutting the route passed under the main road, the bridge being just visible. It passed back again near the isolation hospital. Until the final year, down trains made a lengthy stop here for ticket collecting. (Lens of Sutton)

The 1904 edition reveals that the Station Hotel *backed* onto the road to Woody Bay and so failed in the motoring age as well as the railway era. The cattle market generated little traffic in the final years. There were no cattle wagons on the line, animals being carried in vans with the doors tied open slightly for ventilation - sheep travelled in open trucks covered with nets.

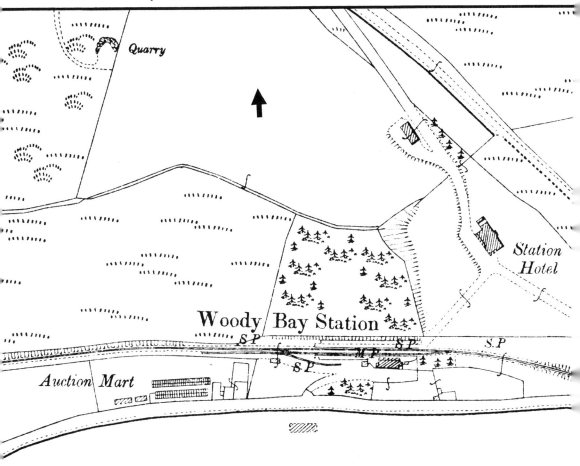

90. A distinctly foreign ambience pervades this scene. The American-built *Lyn* with Norwegian style couplings stands at an Alpine type chalet. At that time, many considered flat bottom rail to be foreign, like the enormous head lamp. (Lens of Sutton)

91. *Yeo* waits with the 3.30pm from Lynton on 8th September 1933, two coaches sufficing for most winter services. The summer holiday season will have just ended. School pupils with season tickets accounted for much of the regular traffic. (K.Nunn/LCGB)

92. The SR altered few of the signals but here they provided a new down home and both up signals, all posts being made from a pair of running rails. The only upper quadrant arm on the line was the up home. Seen here is *Exe*, shunting near the down home in April 1934. When steam heating was required, wagons had to be placed at the rear of the train instead of the front as normal. (Dr.I.C.Allen)

93. A typical Exmoor mist did not deter a passenger in an observation car from recording the porter/signalman returning to the warmth of the station. A few yards of level track between the platforms broke the continuous climb of 1 in 50. The track falls out of sight beyond the points. (D.Cullum coll)

# CAFFYNS HALT

94. The halt was opened in 1907 and was intended to serve a golf course. The bridge carried the lane to West Ilkerton and the platform, seen in July 1925, was on the south side of the line, but there is now no trace of it. (H.C.Casserley)

95. An up train snakes round the curves near the halt on 18th July 1935, headed by *Lew*. Further east, Exmoor is open and unfenced, devoid of the field patterns which made this part of the journey so enjoyable. In August 1952 the build up of flood water between a railway embankment and the road resulted in a surge of water that destroyed Parracombe bridge and killed three people nearby. Lynmouth suffered more seriously at this time. (S.W.Baker)

# LYNTON

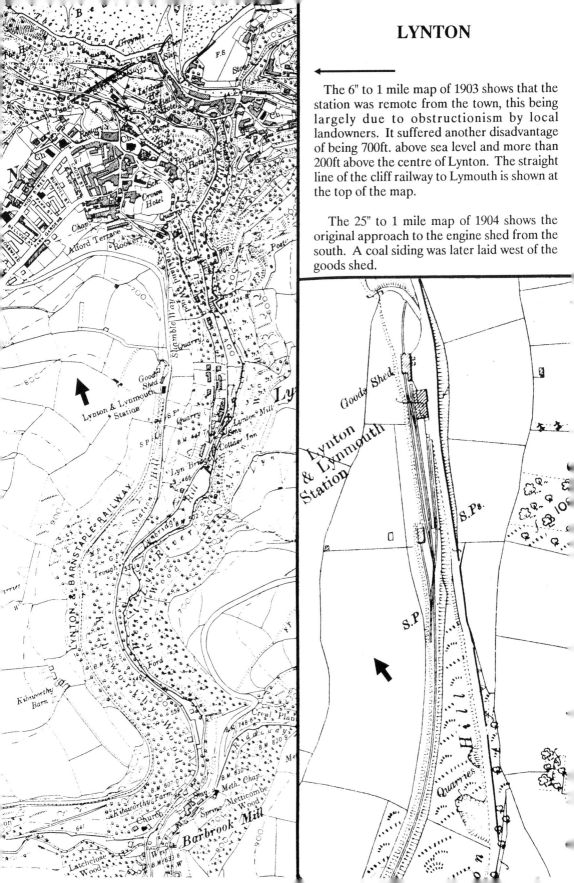

The 6" to 1 mile map of 1903 shows that the station was remote from the town, this being largely due to obstructionism by local landowners. It suffered another disadvantage of being 700ft. above sea level and more than 200ft above the centre of Lynton. The straight line of the cliff railway to Lymouth is shown at the top of the map.

The 25" to 1 mile map of 1904 shows the original approach to the engine shed from the south. A coal siding was later laid west of the goods shed.

96. *Yeo* waits by the newly constructed engine shed shortly before the opening, the patterns on the side tanks being fashionable a way of polishing locomotives at that time. The supplementary side coupling chains soon fell into disuse. (C.G.Maggs coll.)

—M•O. & Co., Ltd.—(98)

# Lynton and Barnstaple Railway. DOWN.

Engine Driver's Report. _28_ day, _September_ 190 _1_ _2-30_ Train.

| STATIONS. | SERVICE TIME. | | | | ACTUAL TIME. | | | | VEHICLES ATTACHED. | | | | | VEHICLES DETACHED. | | REMARKS. |
|---|---|---|---|---|---|---|---|---|---|---|---|---|---|---|---|---|
| | Arrival. | | Departure. | | Arrival. | | Departure. | | Coaches. | Brake Vans. | Goods. | Goods Trucks. Loaded. | | Goods Trucks. | | |
| | H. | M. | H. | M. | H. | M. | H. | M: | | | | Goods, 8 W. | Goods, 4 W. | Empty. | 8 W. | 4 W. | |
| Barnstaple ... ... | | | | | | | 2 | 30 | 2 | 1 | | | 1 | | | | |
| Chelfham ... ... | | | | | 2 | 50 | 2 | 54 | | | | | | | | | |
| Bratton ... ... | | | | | 3 | 5 | 3 | 7 | | | | | | | | | |
| Blackmoor ... ... | | | | | 3 | 25 | 3 | 28 | | | | | | | | 1 | |
| Parrace | | | | | 3 | 39 | 3 | 40 | | | | | | | | | |
| Wooda Bay ... ... | | | | | 3 | 46 | 3 | 48 | | | | | | | | | |
| Lynton ... ... ... | | | | | 4 | 3 | | | | | | | | | | | |
| | | | | | | | | TOTAL | | | | | | | | | |
| | | | | | | | | Time finished duty | | | | | | | | | |

_Y Northcombe_ Driver's Signature.

97. Coach no. 2 is seen prior to the completion of the platform and the loop. This is the vehicle that became a house of prayer and is now at the National Railway Museum. The deep valley of the West Lyn is in the background. The original coach livery was reddish-brown and white, varnished to give high lustre. Lettering was in gold. (R.C.Riley coll.)

99. Although lettered *L&B RAILy LUGGAGE CART*, the service was provided by Tom Jones. Before descending the 1 in 4 gradient to Lynmouth, cast iron skids were secured under the wheels so that the horse dragged the cart down with the wheels motionless. A coach appears to the right of the goods shed. (T.Trickey)

98. The contractor's lightweight track is evident as *Taw* waits with one of the four 1st class observations. Canvas blinds were provided before they were fully glazed. This, and the previous picture, shows the first train on 14th March 1898, two months before the line was opened. (R.C.Riley coll.)

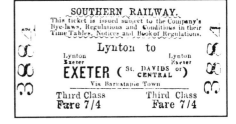

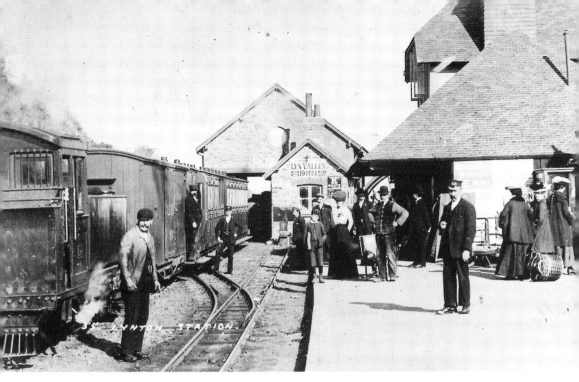

100. *Lyn* stands on the loop with the rear of its train nearly in the goods shed - maybe there were wagons to attach. The Lyn Valley Hotel was largely destroyed in the 1952 Lynmouth disaster (later described). The staff comprised a stationmaster and two porters - three in the summer season. (Lens of Sutton)

**102.** *Yeo* is seen prior to the fitting of steam heating connections. After arrival, locomotives usually ran forward to collect any wagons from the goods shed, then ran round the train before propelling it and incoming wagons into the shed. Originally the starting signals had been on separate posts and the down homes were on one post, one above the other. (Lens of Sutton)

**101.** As passengers chat, we have the opportunity to see that the platform was not rail height or one brick high as often described. At least this was not the case when this photograph was taken on 27th August 1910. (H.D.Hewitt/R.C.Riley)

| | Down. | Week Days. | | | | | | | | | Sn | | Up. | Week Days. | | | | | | | | Suns. | |
|---|---|---|---|---|---|---|---|---|---|---|---|---|---|---|---|---|---|---|---|---|---|---|---|---|
| Miles. | | mrn | K | mrn | mrn | aft | aft | aft | K | aft | K | | Miles. | | mrn | mrn | mrn | aft | K | aft | aft | aft | K | K | K |
| | Barnstaple Town....dep. | 6 18 | 7 0 | 9 0 | 10 15 | 1 33 | 3 25 | 4 30 | 4 55 | 7 50 | 3 50 | | | Lynton and Lynmouth..dep. | 7 18 | 9 20 | 11 13 | 12 42 | 2 a0 | 3 40 | 6 12 | 8 0 | 9 45 | 9 30 | 10 15 |
| 2¼ | Snapper Halt........... | 6 29 | | 9 11 | 10 26 | 1 44 | 3 36 | 4 41 | ... | 8 1 | .... | 1½ | | Caffyns Halt............ | | 9 28 | 11 21 | 12 50 | ... | 3 48 | 6 20 | 8 | 8 | .... | |
| 5 | Chelfham.............. | 6 37 | 7 15 | 9 19 | 10 35 | 1 53 | 3 45 | 4 50 | 5 15 | 8 10 | 4 15 | 2½ | | Woody Bay............. | 7 32 | 9 35 | 11 28 | 12 57 | 2 17 | 3 55 | 6 27 | 8 15 | 10 | 9 47 | 2 32 |
| 8 | Bratton Fleming........ | 6 51 | 7 35 | 9 34 | 10 49 | 2 8 | 3 59 | 5 4 | 5 35 | 8 24 | 4 35 | 4½ | | Parracombe Halt........ | 7 40 | 9 44 | 11 39 | 1 5 | 2 22 | 4 3 | 6 36 | 8 25 | 10 7 | 9 52 | 2 37 |
| 12 | Blackmoor............. | 7 8 | 7 55 | 9 54 | 11 7 | 2 26 | 4 18 | 5 22 | 5 55 | 8 42 | 4 55 | 7½ | | Blackmoor............. | 7 53 | 9 58 | 11 52 | 1 19 | 2 30 | 4 17 | 6 50 | 8 38 | 10 15 | 10 Y0 | 2 45 |
| 14½ | Parracombe Halt........ | 7 22 | 8 3 | 10 13 | 11 21 | 2 40 | 4 33 | 5 36 | 6 2 | 8 56 | 5 3 | 11½ | | Bratton Fleming........ | 8 11 | 10 16 | 12 11 | 1 37 | 2 50 | 4 35 | 7 8 | 9 | 10 35 | 10 20 | 3 5 |
| 16 | Woody Bay............. | 7 31 | 8 | 10 22 | 11 30 | 2 50 | 4 42 | 5 45 | 6 | 9 5 | 5 8 | 14½ | | Chelfham.............. | 8 25 | 10 30 | 12 25 | 1 51 | 3 V10 | 4 49 | 7 22 | 9 15 | 10 V53 | 10 V40 | 3 V25 |
| 17½ | Caffyns Halt........... | 7 42 | .... | 10 39 | 11 39 | 2 59 | 4 51 | 5 53 | ... | 9 13 | .... | 16½ | | Snapper Halt.......... [177 | 8 33 | 10 44 | 12 34 | 2 ... | 5 0 | 7 30 | 9 24 | .... | | |
| 19½ | Lynton and Lynmouth..arr. | 7 51 | 8 25 | 10 39 | 11 48 | 3 8 | 5 0 | 6 2 | 6 25 | 9 22 | 5 25 | 19½ | | Barnstaple Town G 176.arr | 8 46 | 10 56 | 12 46 | 2 14 | 3 20 | 5 12 | 7 42 | 9 36 | 11 0 | 11 0 | 3 45 |

BARNSTAPLE ,TOWN and LYNTON and LYNMOUTH.

| a Lynton Southern National Omnibus Office. | D Barnstaple Junction Station. G Over ¼ mile to Barnstaple Station. | K Southern National Motor Omnibus. V Chelfham Cross. | Y Blackmoor Gate. |
|---|---|---|---|

August 1931

103. Drifting of snow in cuttings presents problems but this unidentifiable engine has won the battle. Under such conditions, many former passengers returned to the railway when the roads were unusable. (E.Northcombe/R.C.Riley)

---

**Lynton and Barnstaple Ry.**

*From* .................................................................

TO

# BLACKMOOR.

---

104. As evident in the picture before last, both platforms were signalled for passenger trains. Seen on 16th July 1935, *Taw* has just arrived in the bay, while *Lew* is ready to depart from the main platform. (S.W.Baker)

105. The remaining photographs were taken in the last few weeks of operation. North of the goods shed the siding terminated in the coal yard, in which one of the two cranes provided by the SR stood on an isolated length of track. (H.F.Wheeller)

106. The permanent way remained in excellent condition to the end. The signal box measured 9x8ft and contained seven levers. The engine shed was open at both ends and little used. The line had been reballasted by the SR, using high quality material from Meldon Quarry on Dartmoor.
(H.F.Wheeller)

107. For some years the station was provided with both bookstall and refreshment room. The upper floor had two bedrooms but the SR decided that the ground floor living rooms were required as offices and built a staff bungalow on the hillside, right.
(H.F.Wheeller)

108. The water column beside *Yeo* was seldom used owing to chronic water shortage at this height and good supplies being available lower down the line. Passengers often arrived to find the toilets closed due to lack of water. On the right is the lamp room and oil store.
(R.C.Riley coll.)

109. *Taw* is seen in the bay platform again, as holidaymakers pass the mail bags. The Royal Mail van is at the end of the platform, which was initially lit by oil and was the only one to be illuminated electrically. Lynmouth was one of the pioneers of hydro electricity, having its own 100 cycle supply from 1890 until 1952. Although Lynton sometimes claims to be the first with public lighting by electricity, Godalming predates it by nine years. (H.F.Wheeller)

110. *Lyn* and *Exe* wait to depart with a long train, with a van in the lead. Shunting at intermediate stations was unpopular with passengers but there was insufficient traffic to justify separate goods trains. The engine shed still had one pair of doors. (H.F.Wheeller)

111. The last train on 29th September 1935 left at 7.55pm as the town band played *Auld Lang Syne* to the accompaniment of a cacophony of detonators. It arrived at Barnstaple at 9.37, 15 minutes late. (R.C.Riley coll.)

112. A 1937 view shows the goods shed before it was converted into two cottages. The chimneys are on the adjacent goods office which was incorporated into one dwelling. Following complaints soon after the opening, a new direct road to Lynton was built and is behind the camera. (S.W.Baker)

113. The boarded-up station master's accommodation is included in this 1937 picture. The combined populations of Lynton and Lynmouth rose from 1641 in 1901 to 2011 in 1931 - no wonder the railway had to be abandoned. The entire population of the district it served was probably little more than 3000, except in the brief holiday season. (S.W.Baker)

→

114. A 1974 photograph from Station Hill reveals a tasteful adaptation for residential purposes. The small windows once served the often-closed toilets. In contrast to the superb view from this location, the FR terminus was surrounded by waste slate tips. Both termini had cable worked inclined railways nearby, each carrying the principal traffic of the district, tourists in the case of Lynton. (N.W.Hearn)

## Traffic Records

The figures are worthy of careful study. At several stations coal and parcel traffic remained fairly steady over the sample years while passengers declined. The season tickets were mainly issued to scholars travelling to Barnstaple, the long journey giving ample time for unscrewing fittings and causing other mischief. Holiday weekly tickets were also included in these figures. Milk traffic was generally shown in gallons after 1931, as the 17 gallon churn was largely displaced by tankers on the main lines that year.

| Lynton | 1928 | 1930 | 1932 | 1934 |
|---|---|---|---|---|
| No. of passenger tickets issued | 11699 | 9505 | 6656 | 5583 |
| No. of season tickets issued | - | 42 | 53 | 67 |
| No. of tickets collected | 30981 | 24646 | 19040 | 19326 |
| No. of telegrams | - | - | - | - |
| Parcels forwarded | 1213 | 1066 | 850 | 1131 |
| Parcels received | 15642 | 15478 | 14274 | 15932 |
| Horses forwarded | - | - | 2 | - |
| Cans of milk forwarded | - | 1 | - | - |
| Cans of milk received | 510 | 497 | 3851 | 5872 |
| General goods forwarded (tons) | 357 | 317 | 266 | 262 |
| General goods received (tons) | 2383 | 2122 | 1775 | 1697 |
| Coal, Coke etc. | 2513 | 2550 | 2717 | 2561 |
| Other minerals forwarded | - | - | - | - |
| Other minerals received | 191 | 329 | 324 | 243 |
| Trucks livestock forwarded | 17 | 3 | 2 | 5 |
| Trucks livestock received | 27 | 18 | 7 | 3 |
| Lavatory pennies | 2532 | 2148 | 2052 | 1716 |

| Chelfham | 1928 | 1930 | 1932 | 1934 |
|---|---|---|---|---|
| No. of passenger tickets issued | 3387 | 2708 | 2718 | 2490 |
| No. of season tickets issued | 1 | 6 | 2 | 6 |
| No. of tickets collected | 3581 | 2727 | 2826 | 2552 |
| No. of telegrams | - | - | - | - |
| Parcels forwarded | 442 | 714 | 546 | 665 |
| Parcels received | 128 | 145 | 164 | 236 |
| Horses forwarded | - | - | - | - |
| Cans of milk forwarded | - | - | - | - |
| Cans of milk received | - | - | - | - |
| General goods forwarded (tons) | 10 | 23 | 12 | 16 |
| General goods received (tons) | 26 | 34 | 17 | 12 |
| Coal, Coke etc. | 23 | 31 | 18 | 18 |
| Other minerals forwarded | - | - | - | - |
| Other minerals received | - | 6 | 12 | 7 |
| Trucks livestock forwarded | - | - | - | - |
| Trucks livestock received | - | - | - | - |
| Lavatory pennies | - | - | - | - |

| Bratton Fleming | 1928 | 1930 | 1932 | 1934 |
|---|---|---|---|---|
| No. of passenger tickets issued | 4446 | 4243 | Tickets issued | |
| No. of season tickets issued | 1 | 8 | by guard | |
| No. of tickets collected | 4700 | 3846 | 2893 | 2556 |
| No. of telegrams | - | - | - | - |
| Parcels forwarded | 948 | 784 | 366 | 770 |
| Parcels received | 279 | 337 | 335 | 384 |
| Horses forwarded | - | - | - | - |
| Cans of milk forwarded | - | - | - | - |
| Cans of milk received | - | - | - | - |
| General goods forwarded (tons) | 7 | 6 | 6 | 9 |
| General goods received (tons) | 48 | 40 | 38 | 29 |
| Coal, Coke etc. | | - | - | - |
| Other minerals forwarded | - | - | - | - |
| Other minerals received | - | 2 | 55 | - |
| Trucks livestock forwarded | - | 1 | - | - |
| Trucks livestock received | - | - | - | - |
| Lavatory pennies | - | - | - | - |

| Blackmoor | 1928 | 1930 | 1932 | 1934 |
|---|---|---|---|---|
| No. of passenger tickets issued | 6515 | 5237 | 4241 | 4025 |
| No. of season tickets issued | 20 | 34 | 47 | 27 |
| No. of tickets collected | 8571 | 6595 | 4927 | 4654 |
| No. of telegrams | - | - | - | 1 |
| Parcels forwarded | 480 | 1076 | 793 | 304 |
| Parcels received | 782 | 772 | 841 | 741 |
| Horses forwarded | - | - | - | - |
| Cans of milk forwarded | 302 | 477 | 76 | 54 |
| Cans of milk received | - | - | - | - |
| General goods forwarded (tons) | 65 | 49 | 52 | 50 |
| General goods received (tons) | 278 | 718 | 597 | 345 |
| Coal, Coke etc. | 120 | 185 | 73 | 36 |
| Other minerals forwarded | - | - | - | - |
| Other minerals received | 75 | 293 | 164 | 184 |
| Trucks livestock forwarded | 8 | 5 | - | - |
| Trucks livestock received | 1 | 1 | - | 12 |
| Lavatory pennies | - | 252 | 288 | 192 |

| Woody Bay | 1928 | 1930 | 1932 | 1934 |
|---|---|---|---|---|
| No. of passenger tickets issued | 2501 | 2186 | 1499 | 1790 |
| No. of season tickets issued | - | 11 | 2 | - |
| No. of tickets collected | 6447 | 4651 | 3463 | 3784 |
| No. of telegrams | - | - | - | 37 |
| Parcels forwarded | 333 | 237 | 194 | 183 |
| Parcels received | 854 | 849 | 778 | 964 |
| Horses forwarded | - | - | - | - |
| Cans of milk forwarded | 183 | 65 | 10 | - |
| Cans of milk received | - | - | - | - |
| General goods forwarded (tons) | 26 | 20 | 15 | 17 |
| General goods received (tons) | 303 | 332 | 255 | 166 |
| Coal, Coke etc. | 362 | 494 | 493 | 380 |
| Other minerals forwarded | - | - | - | - |
| Other minerals received | 309 | 269 | 131 | 200 |
| Trucks livestock forwarded | 11 | 1 | - | - |
| Trucks livestock received | 2 | 5 | - | - |
| Lavatory pennies | | | | |

# LYNTON & LYNMOUTH
# CLIFF RAILWAY

115. The wealthy publisher, Sir George Newnes, financed the construction of this line from his home town of Lynton, the gauge being 3ft 9ins and the length 287yds. It opened in 1890 and has operated without accident ever since, only closing briefly for maintenance. The higher portion of the car bodies have since been rebuilt using timber from a wrecked ship and from Lynton's disused signal posts. (D.Cullum coll.)

116. A 1935 view from Lynton station includes both overbridges and both ropes, one being a duplicate in event of the failure of the other, but both are tensioned equally. The bodies were mounted on wheels and were run off the flat decks when sea-borne freight was conveyed from Lynmouth to Lynton. Motor cars unable to negotiate the 1 in 4 gradient to Lynmouth were carried on the flat decks in the 1920s and again in 1952, following the flood disaster on 15th August in which 34 lives and 132 vehicles were lost. The flood followed over 9ins of rain in 24 hours and caused the destruction of 28 bridges, many of which formed dams when blocked by trees, boulders and carcases. When the bridges failed, they released a tidal wave of water which was up to 24ft deep where the two rivers meet in Lynmouth. (S.W.Baker)

117. The wedge shaped tank at the base of each car is filled with water at the top station, and at the commencement of each journey, the driver of the lower car releases water from his tank causing the heavier one at the top to pull his car up. (L&LCR)

October 1911

FOOT BRAKE PEDAL

WATER DISCHARGE
PEDAL

ACCUMULATOR

GOVERNOR
CONTROLLING
FOOT BRAKE

FOOT BRAKE

GRIP BRAKE

FOOT BRAKE GRIP
PRESSURE

118.   The hydraulic braking system is water
filled, the pump to generate pressure being
operated by the running wheels.   The
operating rams apply pressure to blocks on the
rail head (lower left), while others operate the
mild steel grip brakes on each side of the rail
head.   The automatic governer is driven by the
inner chain (left), while the long one is
connected to weights (top left) and the driver's
control wheel, visible in the previous
photograph. (L&LCR)

119.   The single buffer between the wheels
comes to rest on a hydraulic buffer, which is
claimed to be the prototype for the larger units
later installed at many main line termini.
Indeed, the cliff railway's water balance
principle was once a pioneer design, copied at
many locations in Britain and abroad.
(V.Mitchell)

July 1921

120. At Lynmouth's station waiting room on 29th April 1992 is Mr Bob Jones, managing director of the railway and grandson of the builder of the line (also Bob Jones) who in addition built the L&BR's three northern stations. The builder's brother was Tom Jones who operated the bus services to and from the GWR at Minehead. The Jones family thus have a unique place in Devon's railway history. (V.Mitchell)

**MP** *Middleton Press*

Easebourne Lane, Midhurst, West Sussex. GU29 9AZ
Tel: (0730) 813169   Fax: (0730) 812601

## Other West Country albums -

*Branch Lines to Exmouth*
*Branch Line to Lyme Regis*
*Branch Lines to Seaton and Sidmouth*
*Branch Line to Swanage to 1992*
*Branch Lines around Weymouth*
*Bournemouth to Weymouth*
*Exeter to Barnstaple*
*Salisbury to Yeovil*
*Yeovil to Exeter*
*Yeovil to Dorchester*

## Somerset and Dorset Railway albums -

*Bath to Evercreech Junction*
*Bournemouth to Evercreech Junction*
*Burnham to Evercreech Junction*

## Other narrow gauge albums -

*Branch Lines around Portmadoc 1923 - 46*
*Branch Line to Southwold*

**All the albums listed are by Vic Mitchell and Keith Smith
and are in similar format, each containing
120 photographs and numerous maps.**

**Write or telephone for our complete list of
railway, tramway and waterway books.**